I Have A Father

Sharinatl Q. Ingram-Arrington

HOV
PUBLISHING

HOV Publishing a division of HOV, LLC.
www.hovpub.com
hopeofvision@gmail.com

Cover Design: Hope of Vision Designs
Editor: Melissa Zraik

Contact the Author, Sharinatl Q. Ingram-Arrington at:
shonieworld@gmail.com

For further information regarding special discounts on bulk purchases, please reply to www.hovpub.com

ISBN Paperback: 978-1-942871-89-7

First Edition
10 9 8 7 6 5 4 3 2 1

Printed in the United States of America

I Have A Father

Sharinatl Q. Ingram-Arrington

Dedication

This book is dedicated to:

Donald Mays, my biological father,
The Rev. Dr. Lee A. Arrington, my spiritual father,
and father-in-law, Bishop Raymond A. Jenkins, with
special sentiments in loving memory,
Larry D. Basnight, my dad,
Bunyon D. Tyson, my brother, and
Bobby E. Arrington, my beloved husband.

To my daughters, whom I love dearly, Shaneta,
Azeere, Azhenay, and Serenity—don't you ever
forget that you have a Father in Heaven who will be
there for you always.

To my dear mother, Marilyn P. Ingram-Basnight,
who taught me, by example, to be a strong woman.

Thank you to my mother-in-law, Patricia A. Motley-
Arrington for raising my loving husband to be a
great father.

Special Endorsement

This is written and dedicated to my beautiful wife:

There is no one on this earth like you. Nobody looks like you, dresses like you, acts like you. You know it's true; nobody has your courage to speak your words. You get that look in your eyes and have the nerve. It doesn't take a genius to figure out that you are so different. Everyone has their flaws, but to me, you are so perfect. I just want to be with you. I don't care what I have to do. Walls in front of me, I'm going through. There is no one on this earth like you.

You were created just for me. I am the world's envy because there is only one of you. There is no one on this earth like you. Now I know!

Love Your Husband,
Bob Arrington

Contents

Foreword

When I think of my close friend Sharinatl, she is not only a wonderful person and a trailblazer but a woman of strength. Throughout twenty years of friendship, Sharinatl has endured, persevered, and overcome life's most complex situations that seemed impossible to overcome. I have witnessed many miracles in her life, which resulted in victory and restoration, through prayer, an integral part of her journey.

Sharinatl writes from the depth of her knowledge, trials, tribulations, and revelations from God.

Watching her excavate the word of God encourages me and increases my expectation of where the Lord is taking her. I'm blessed and honored to be part of her life. It gives me great comfort and joy to fulfill the Lord's commissions to "…pray ye for one another…" (James 5:16, KJV) and "bear ye one another's burdens..." (Galatians 6:2, KJV).

I can think of no better way to truly cherish friendship than by praying consistently, for prayer is priceless. I desire that she experience God's blessings and His grace continually, and this book is transformative to all who read it. I hope you're ready to connect or re-connect with your heavenly Father. This word from the Lord is for all to read and receive. Evangelist Sharinatl Arrington my friend, I love you.

Your Forever Sister & Friend
Pastor Tonia Jenkins

Chapter 1

A Relationship

Relationships form when individuals communicate or interact with each other. Our experiences and encounters with others shape our ability to socialize within the relationship. Moreover, the quality of those experiences, whether good or bad, can have a positive or negative effect on how we interact with humanity in general. During my first year of college, one of my courses covered nature versus nurture related to relationships. The professor, who was a man of God, presented scientific studies by several psychologists that focused on genetics or prior relationships as a determining factor of a person's behavior. This lesson opened my eyes, spiritually and mentally. It caused me to assess the wellness of my relationships from this perspective.

For me, growing up, I had a hard time trusting anyone that was not a part of my inner circle. It was generally easy for me to hold conversations with family members. Still, I struggled to find the right words to say if specific topics came up. I am blessed to say that I grew up in a home full of love, but the dysfunction was still present.

During my childhood, my father was not present. I knew who he was and still have memories of the special things he would do for me during the holidays, but I don't recall having a relationship with him. I would only see him very briefly to retrieve gifts, hugs, kisses, and exchange a few words. I can remember feeling happy anticipating his arrival, but

I instantly felt sad after his departure. I do remember saying to my father, "I love you." However, I was not old enough to understand precisely what those words meant. I knew of him but didn't know him, but I will get deeper into that in another chapter.

The emotions of becoming very excited and then sad became very familiar to me after a while. Eventually, when the short visits ended altogether, I was left feeling depressed. This separation was unhealthy for me. I missed my father and often wondered if he missed me. As time passed, the thoughts and questions of, "*Did I do something wrong? Does he still love me? What happened to him? Will I ever see him again?*" became my frequent companions. I was experiencing separation anxiety, which no one ever knew because I kept these thoughts to myself. Because my mother never mentioned him, neither did I.

During my elementary school years, my mom was a very active parent. She served on the Parent's Association (PTA) at the school I attended, spearheading fundraisers and hosting talent shows. Serving as an inspirational mentor to the children, she knew how to help discover and perfect their talents. Using the tools of singing and dancing, she brought out the best in us. I performed in all the shows with great pride. However, I always felt sad that my father's presence was never there. I thought I couldn't tell my mom how I felt because she was so proud and happy, I didn't want to kill her joy.

I was an honor roll student with excellent grades and made sure I was always well behaved. After all, my mother was in school most of the time. I remember feeling a deep pain of disappointment on graduation day. Walking across the stage to receive my diploma, everyone was cheering. Yet, I was crying inside because once again, my father did not appear. The silence of my agony was torturous. However, I learned how to act like nothing was wrong. Perhaps if I had shared my concerns, someone could have helped me to get through what I was feeling.

When experiencing a tough time, having someone to talk to can make a big difference. Communicating with others is a healthy way of releasing things you may need to say to cope with the situation. However, we must be mindful of whom we share our concerns. Having a good relationship with people that care about you is crucial and enhances your ability to be social. Parents can provide the nurturing that is essential for developing healthy relationships. Every child needs to feel secure while growing up in the world. The absence of my father stripped me of the security that I needed.

Going through this alone was not the right choice. I was very introverted, and that worked against me. I became comfortable having conversations with my inner self and was often left feeling worse about the situation. It is not easy to live life when you feel like something or someone is missing mostly if you know their existence is vital to your well-being. The absence of a father can hurt a child psychologically. Family unity is weakened without the presence of a father – the person God ordained as the head of the household. God intended the father to serve as the protector and provider. The absence of a father also harms the physical strength of the family – leaving it vulnerable and subject to exploitation by the enemy. However, there is hope because God knows what we need. He can be the father that you need in your life.

~Prayer~

Father, in the name of Jesus, I pray that you would hear my cry. Create in me a clean heart and let no malice interfere with my prayer. Lord, help me to overcome the rejection that I have experienced in my life. Cancel the effects that rejection has had on my heart and purify me from the residue that tries to linger and influence my thoughts. Help me to remember that you have never rejected me, and you never will. Help me to know that everyone that left me pushed me closer to you. Thank you, Lord, for everyone that walked away from me that was only meant to be in my life for a season. Amen.

Chapter 2

Rejection

When faced with rejection, the need for filling a void becomes apparent through a lack of self-esteem and how we measure our self-worth and confidence. I found myself silently searching for my father and the love I needed from him. I wanted to hear him say, "I love you." Rejection can trigger the thought that no one loved me. Mentally, I associated love with words instead of actions. While I had the love of my family, I didn't recognize it. Instead, I was focused on the love that I wasn't getting from my father. So, I started out on my journey, searching for love.

I found that having a healthy relationship with my biological father increased my chances, as with many women, identifying good or bad relationships with men. A woman's father can set the tone for her expectations from a man she is dating or help her determine the kind of man she wants to marry. On the other hand, when a woman experiences a lousy relationship with her father, it can cause her to seek for someone to fulfill her void and pain. It could also lead her down a path of having bad encounters with men. She may even tend to attract men that prey on weak women because her vulnerability is visible. I entered into relationships seeking love from men because I didn't feel loved by my father.

This became a cycle of rejection and caused more damage mentally when I became disappointed. With each rejection and failure, my heart was broken into a thousand pieces. However, I came to realize that my heart needed to heal for me to recognize what love was. The healing process began when I came into a relationship with God. His word revealed the true meaning of love and changed my life forever. I learned "for God so loved the world, that he gave his only begotten son, that whosoever believeth in him should not perish, but have everlasting life" (John 3:16, KJV). This is the source of true love, God's *agape* love!

Love is about sacrifice, and it will not allow you to be selfish. God sacrificed his son for us while we were yet in despair because he loves us. This is the act of an amazing father, a good father who will always make sacrifices when his children need him, no matter the cost. He didn't have to do it, but love made a choice for Him. These truths are borne out in 1 Corinthians 13:4-5 (KJV), which states, "Love is patient, love is kind. It does not envy, it does not boast, it is not proud. It does not dishonor others, it is not self-seeking, it is not easily angered, it keeps no record of wrongs."

This was a light that pulled me out of a dark place. In the process of the truth being revealed, I had to accept the fact that the men I dated didn't love me. This was a hard pill to swallow; nonetheless, it set me on the path to really living. I was being healed in one area of my life, but there were levels of pain that needed attention. Now that I knew what love was, I tried to force someone to love me. I was failing my love quest, and I knew it.

Oh, how my heart began to yearn for love even more because I knew that love was the antidote I needed. While I understood what God's love was, and what it could do for me, it was hard to allow the power of His love to work in my life. I wanted a physical love as well to feed the desires of my flesh.

Not ready spiritually to embrace the fullness of God's love, I rejected His power that my life sorely needed. Unknowingly, I became both the rejected and the rejector. Mentally, I was an emotional wreck. Rejection morphed into multiple issues, including low self-esteem, distrust, loneliness, and feelings of abandonment. I lost faith in love and began to feel like I would never feel its beauty, but most of all, that I didn't deserve to be loved.

Howbeit, all was not lost. In our time of troubles, God uses divine intervention to draw us closer to himself, whereby our needs are met. Scripture tells us that God is a rewarder of them that diligently seek him (Hebrews 11:6, KJV). Would I have searched for him if I was not looking for my biological father? Probably not, but there is a distinct possibility that I would have gone through life not recognizing there was a void that needed to be filled. I often say if I never went through anything, what would I need God for?

There are some things we want in life, and then there are some things we need. I knew I needed a father who could provide the missing elements of guidance and protection – the cushion of security that every little girl needs comfort to feel secure. Although my mother was always there for me, and my stepfather was great, I could not shake the fact that my biological father was not in my life. In some cases, the father is frequently absent from the home due to death, incarceration, drug addictions, or other mishaps. Nevertheless, it is still very painful for a child to endure the absence of a father.

Although there may be a legitimate reason for not being there, it doesn't change the results of how it could affect the child's experience. In my case, as with many others, this void resulted in a broken heart. However, this pain is not incurable. God, who is our Father, gives us that everlasting love and comfort we are missing because of the absence of our biological father (2 Thessalonians 2:16-17). And through the relationship with Him, our path is established with good works through His word (Psalm 119:133 NKJV). It is then we can learn how to love based on our relationship with God.

~Prayer~

God, I thank you for all the pain that I have endured. Lord, I confess that I allowed the pain to distract me for moments in my life. Please forgive me for the errors of my ways and allow me to see that pain comes in life only to help us understand that we can overcome trials and tribulations with the victory.

Chapter 3

Driven By Pain

Painful Decisions

As I look back, I realize I allowed pain to push me in the wrong direction. Pain influenced my decisions, which were often flawed and caused embarrassing memories. Perhaps if I received the healing necessary for growth and maturity early in life, I would not have been driven by pain to make the following, regretful decision.

At the age of sixteen, I found myself in bed with someone I thought loved me, resulting in the loss of my virginity, my precious jewel, just like that. As I reflect on that night, I remember it with great clarity – lying down, feeling one way, and getting up feeling disgusted! *Why did I do that? I wasn't ready!* But I couldn't change what happened. It didn't feel good at all. I only did it because I wanted my boyfriend to like me. At the time, I thought that if I didn't submit to my boyfriend, he would walk away from me just like my father did. I know it may sound ridiculous, but that is what I believed. Little did I know that having sex was not going to keep my boyfriend in my life forever. *How could I look in the mirror at myself after this?* If my mother was planning a sweet sixteen, I wasn't deserving of it. With one decision I made, I was changed. I wasn't sweet at all.

After many years of not seeing my father, he suddenly appeared. Eventually, I began spending many nights out without my mother's approval – even running away from home. There I was embracing the love I thought I needed. He showed up, and I was perplexed. *"What is he doing here,"* I whispered to myself? I stood in the doorway of my boyfriend's house, holding a conversation with the man that had abandoned me. *"Oh no, he has no right to be here,"* that's how I felt. *"Did he show up to take back love from me once again?"* Instead of questioning him, I pretended to listen to what he had to say. Once again, he was gone as quickly as he had come, and I felt ten times worse.

I'm sure that my father had good intentions and thought he had done something great by showing up. I didn't need him to just show up; I needed him to stay. I smoked marijuana immediately after he left to tune out his sudden appearance and disappearance. Immediately after he left, I resorted to smoking marijuana to tune out his sudden appearance and disappearance. After all, his visit was a blur anyway. He knew how to walk in and out of my life like a magician swiftly doing a trick without my eyes catching the steps he took to fool me.

The inconsistency of our interactions was not good for my emotional state. Although I loved him, I realized that this relationship wasn't healthy for me. Consequently, I made up my mind that I did not want to see him again. If this was what our relationship was going to be like, I didn't want it. In fact, I didn't need it. It was strange that even though he was hurting me, I still loved him. His actions just didn't equal what God our Father had promised: "I will never leave thee, nor forsake thee" (Hebrews 13:5, KJV). God, the promise keeper, and comforter loves us, knows what and when we need him, will always be there. Now I understand that my biological father may not have known how much I needed him in my life.

No one really knew what I was going through. I guarded and held this secret close to my heart, and away from others whom I was not sure would understand how I was feeling – ashamed! Growing up in my household, my siblings had their father within reach every day and night while I yearned for my father's love. I was blessed because my stepfather never mistreated me, yet I wasn't satisfied. Instead of appreciating the father I had in my life, I was pouting about the one I didn't have.

Many of you may be able to relate to this. I encourage whoever is reading this to thank God for what and who you have in your life. Don't dwell on what you want but focus on the fact that God always supplies your needs. I'm not suggesting that children don't need their fathers. However, if you do not have your father in your life, God can satisfy that void, mitigating the pain. Often times, God will send someone in your life to act as a surrogate for the father who is missing.

Nevertheless, I often asked myself, *"Why couldn't I have a relationship with my father like my siblings?"* I think it would probably be best to ask, *"Why didn't my father love me as my sibling's father loved them?"* When you go through pain secretly, it leaves room for the enemy to play tricks with your mind—answering your questions with lies and responding to your pain with painful answers. For years, the enemy caused me to believe no one loved me. He would whisper things to me like, *"You are ugly, and nobody wants you,"* which caused me to become hopeless. The enemy's intention was to keep me from having a relationship with God so that I would not be set free, healed, and delivered.

The pain I was feeling interfered with my productivity at school and building healthy relationships with my peers. I camouflaged my pain with fake smiles and hid behind the characteristics of being shy and introverted. I skipped class for months until I decided to drop out of high school altogether. My life spiraled out of control. *"How was I going to overcome this unwanted trial and cycle of pain?* I didn't know nor try to be set free! I was going through life in pain with no cure. Further down, I sunk into the valley of despair, a victim swaddled in comfort.

~Prayer~

Father God, in the name of Jesus, allow me to grow through my mistakes and the pain that has presented itself in my life. Teach me to become victorious in what I am going through. Push me into the new life that you have for me after the pain. I need you to touch me and heal me from the pain and wounds of my afflictions. Thank you in advance for all that you are doing in my life. Amen.

Chapter 4

Growing Pains

At an early age, I became pregnant with my firstborn child. I was scared and didn't know how I would be as a mother. Two weeks after finding out I was pregnant, the baby's father was arrested and sentenced to ten years in jail. I had no clue how I was going to take care of this baby. This couldn't be happening. First, I grew up without my father, and now my child would experience the same pain. Throughout my pregnancy, I attended church faithfully with the realization I needed help.

Somehow, I began to take small steps out of my gloom and darkness.

After my daughter was born, I did what I thought was best. Because I didn't want my daughter to grow up not knowing her father, I tried to take control of the situation to make sure she didn't. So, I would take her to visit him, which was contrary to my mother's wishes and against my better judgment. It took me a few years to realize what I was exposing my daughter to, but I continued to take her even though I felt uncomfortable.

One day, I looked at a picture taken at the prison, and I didn't like what I saw. This wasn't fair to her. What kind of memories had I created for her? Again, the feeling of shame overtook me. I thought about how she might feel with the memories and pictures that I was compiling. The images were a clear reflection of bondage. The enemy desires for the children of God to be in bondage. However, Jesus came so that we might be free from bondage and have life more abundantly (John 10:10 KJV).

The pain you may endure should not be a tool used to imprison you nor alter your ability to be your best. It should not impair your ability to make the right decisions. Instead, it should be the circumstance drives and motivates you to rise and be victorious. At the time, however, I was not thinking about overcoming it. I made myself comfortable by adapting to the situation I was in. Both my daughter and I were trapped in a cycle of pain with unpleasant experiences just to cope. How easy it is to include others in our misery!

Even though I couldn't trust men, I continuously allowed myself to be ensnared in toxic relationships. At the age of thirty-three, I was a single, broken-hearted woman raising four children who also did not have a father in the home. I frequently referred to my household as the home of the fatherless. I did not realize what I was speaking over my children and me. The pain I experienced was not only for myself but for my children as well. Knowing it could harm them, I thought to myself, this is not fair. At that point, I had a nervous breakdown. I was so overwhelmed that it overtook me.

The enemy had knocked me down to my lowest point and the darkest moment in my life. I locked myself in my room and prayed constantly. On my knees, I cried out and pleaded with the Lord to help me. I found comfort in music by Donnie McClurkin entitled, "Live in London." This DVD ministered to my spirit while I was secluded in my room for a week. I only came out to attend to personal needs, drink water, but I do not recall eating anything.

During this experience, I didn't know that God allowed this to happen so He could deliver me. I became aware that He was there for me. Instead of grieving about the absence of my biological father, I called on God, the Father of all fathers. It was then I realized, "In my distress, I called upon the LORD, and cried unto my God: he heard my voice out of his temple, and my cry came before him, even into his ears. Psalm 18:6 KJV."

I endured bondage and cyclical pain and thought there was not a place of refuge away from pain. Spiritual growth was happening, but I did not know it at the time. Psalm 46 states God is our refuge and strength, a very present help in trouble. No matter what the situation, God can break the chains of bondage, set you free, and give you peace of mind. My mind was troubled, but once I gave it to the Lord, I began to heal in a way I had never experienced before. It was time for me to let go and live my life with liberty.

~Prayer~

Most gracious God, I come knowing that I am need of Your healing power. Please, Lord, heal me. I do not want to hurt about this anymore. I have held on to this pain longer than I should have. Today, I am giving it to you. Heal me, Lord; I know you can.

Chapter 5

Healing

"But he was wounded for our transgressions, he was bruised for our iniquities: the chastisement of our peace was upon him; and with his stripes we are healed."

Isaiah 53:5 KJV

I'm sure you have heard the saying, "time can heal all wounds." I don't believe that at all. Time doesn't heal wounds. It merely allows you to move on during your pain comfortably. If time could heal hurt and pain, why are so many suffering from what they endured as a child growing up, and who long will it take to let go? Time shows you that life goes on despite what you are going through.

The enemy desires for God's children to be permanently paralyzed by pain. But know this, your sad story can have a happy ending. You have committed yourself to pain long enough, and now it is time for you to commit yourself to a life full of God's joy and peace. Once you embrace God the Father, He will heal all wounds and pain deep in your heart and soul. Refocus your search for your biological father onto the Spiritual Father, who is waiting to usher you into your destiny. I am a witness that you can live without your biological father, but you need the Father.

If you are raising a child(ren) without their father, teach them about the heavenly Father and His power. Teach them how to pray to their heavenly Father using the example found in Matthew 6:9-13 (NIV), which states, "This, then, is how you should pray:

Our Father in heaven, hallowed be your name, your kingdom come, your will be done, on earth as it is in heaven. Give us today our daily bread. And forgive us our debts, as we also have forgiven our debtors. And lead us not into temptation, but deliver us from the evil one." If they are introduced to God the Father, they will not have to search for a father who is not there or does not want to be found.

Holding a grudge against a missing father does not help but will cause pain to increase by continually reminding of their absence. I made up my mind to believe that God's love could sustain me, and His power could allow me to release my pain. It was then, God became the Father I never had, who holds and comforts me in His arms. He will do the same for you!

Do not be fooled by saying, "I don't need a father" – that is just your pain talking. Let God's strength, healing, and truth be revealed to you. Do not be deceived by the lies of the enemy. Everyone needs a father. When you accept the Lord as your Father, the victory is not always right around the corner. You must move forward, step by step, because the enemy will try to do everything in his weak power to prevent or destroy your relationship with the Father. The enemy will tell whisper, "you are damaged goods, permanently paralyzed by pain, just another damsel in distress without a chance of rescue." But these statements are all lies! Allow God to step in and fight every battle, overcoming every obstacle along your journey in life.

Healing can occur for you, but first, there are a few things that you should consider:

1. Recognize that you need healing,
2. Believe that you can receive healing,
3. You have to want to be healed.

Healing Scriptures

Psalm 34:19 KJV

"Many are the afflictions of the righteous: but the Lord delivereth him out of them all."

Jeremiah 17:14 NIV

"Heal me, Lord, and I will be healed; save me and I will be saved, for you are the one I praise."

Jeremiah 30:17 NIV

"But I will restore you to health and heal your wounds,' declares the Lord."

~Prayer~

Father, in the name of Jesus, I pray that the person that is reading this will receive You in their life as the true and living God. Reveal to him or her that You are the Father and denounce all doubts and lies they have been exposed to.

Chapter 6

The Father

We must understand how we are connected and related to God, whom we call Abba, our Father. In Romans 8:15 (KJV), the Holy Spirit declares that we are God's children and joint heirs with Christ; therefore, we can call God Abba Father! He is the good, faithful, and perfect Father who will be "…with you always, even until the end of the world" (Matthew 28:20, KJV).

I realize I'm not the only one who grew up without a father, but I still long for the love of a father. You may feel that you have been cheated out of what you deserve and need. If you are on a quest looking for love or need a void to be filled, you don't have to search anymore. Build a relationship with the Father; He will heal the brokenness of your heart. Psalm 147:3 (KJV) proclaims, "He healeth the broken in heart, and bindeth up their wounds," because he is the Father who cares about you and everything you are going through. So, let Him into your heart and your situation, so your healing can begin. If you are in pain that is disrupting your life, despair not because your Father is near. The Prophet Isaiah admonished us to seek the Father, and when you do, you will find Him (55:6, NIV). Moreover, when you find Him, "Cast...all your [pain] upon him; for he careth for you" (1 Peter 5:7, KJV).

God, the Father, has broad shoulders that can bare you up irrespective of the situation you become entangled in because He is dependable and always there. He does what my biological father could not do relating to protection, restoration, healing, and, most of all, guidance. When you are uncertain and do not know what to do or which way to go, Proverbs 3:5-6 (KJV) instructs us to "Trust in the LORD with all thine heart; and lean not unto thine own understanding. In all thy ways acknowledge him, and he shall direct thy paths." Even when you experience setbacks, God will lead and guide you back onto the path, and His perfect will for your life. You can be assured, "…that all things work together for good to them that love God, to those who are the called according to His purpose" (Romans 8:28, KJV).

I decided to trust God in the midst of my pain, and He has never failed me. He can do the same thing for you. If you allow the power of God to work in your life, you will have relief from your distress. Decide today that you no longer want to be held down. Choose to seek healing instead of accepting the pain that is present in your life.

~Prayer~

Lord, I come to You as humble as I know-how. I pray that You would create in me a clean heart and renew a right spirit within me. I pray that You would allow my heart to forgive all that have hurt me and caused me pain.

Chapter 7

Forgiveness

For you to heal, it is imperative to forgive. I forgave my father for not being in my life the way I wanted him to. During a conversation I had with my father, crying, he spoke sincerely from his heart, giving me insight into the guilt he felt. It was at that moment that I was made aware of how he was also affected. I knew that it took courage to admit what he had done wrong. He apologized, and I felt blessed to have heard the words, "I am sorry." I told him that I forgave him and was grateful that he shared this information with me because it changed my perspective of him. Today, I can accept that my father is not a bad man because he wasn't there for me. Dwelling on the past was not profitable for either of us! I love my father, and I thank God for him. The blood that binds us together can never be broken; neither can the physical distance diminish our love.

While some fathers will never apologize to their children even when they know they should, some will never have that opportunity to say, "I am sorry." My heart goes out in prayer for the fathers who squandered opportunities to make this confession to their children. If you are one of those children who never received an apology from your father, you can still walk in forgiveness. We know this to be true because Colossians 3:13 (NIV) states, "Bear with each other and forgive one another if any of you has a grievance against someone. Forgive as the Lord forgave you." The words of this scripture nullify past hurts whereby you are healed, comforted by God, and move on with your life. Don't let the absence of these spoken words affect you any longer.

Forgiveness between my father and I was a powerful moment, whereby the enemy's plan was defeated. The devil wanted us to be bound by the cares of this life, circumstances, trials, and tribulations. However, He is powerless if we take on the mentality of being overcomers. Romans 12:2 (KJV) states the mind of an overcomer is accomplished by not thinking as the world does. But instead, you can be transformed from a world of hurt and pain by renewing your mind through God's Word. You will then prove God's power in your life and perform the perfect will of God by forgiving, just as I forgave my father!

Unforgiveness leads to bitterness, anger, and even malice – stealing our joy and peace. The Apostle Paul cautions us to put these feelings away and "be kind to one another, tenderhearted, forgiving one another, as God in Christ forgave you" (Ephesians 4:31-32, ESV). Jesus is our example, who encourages us not to focus on the wrong others inflict upon you. Even when faced with the most unimaginable pain, Jesus forgave those who mocked and put him to death. He realized they were fully aware of what they were doing (Luke 23:34, KJV). Likewise, I chose to forgive my father because he did not hurt me intentionally. Although the enemy wanted me to believe that he did, the truth was revealed to me, and it set me free from that lie.

We cannot change what others have done to us, but we can change how it affects us. I decided to write this book to encourage and set free those who have difficulty forgiving their father. You are not fatherless; God is your Father. Psalm 27:10 (KJV) reminds us, "When my father and my mother forsake me, then the LORD will take me up (Psalm 27:10 KJV)." I learned, through faith, that God guards this and other promises He made us with great jealousy – nothing will cause His promises to change. He is a promise keeper, "not one word of all the promises that the Lord made....[will] fail...(Joshua 21:45,

ESV) nor does He lie or change His mind (Numbers 23:19, ESV).

Your faith will lead you to believe in the Father who is in heaven, whom you cannot see with your eyes. Again, we reflect on God's word to strengthen our faith, for Hebrews 11:1 (NIV) states, "Now faith is confidence in what we hope for and assurance about what we do not see." To accomplish this, study, read, listen to the word of God, which will enable you to use it accurately and effectively in your life (2 Timothy 2:15, NIV). The word of God will give you power to take control of what has been controlling you. Start the process by forgiving whoever offended you to move into your space of victory.

Forgiveness brings freedom. It gives you the liberty to live life without regrets. Holding on to the hurt and pain will only keep bad memories alive that cripple your stability. Embrace the joy of the Lord, which is found in His word, because it is your strength (Nehemiah 8:10, KJV). Remember, "...whenever you stand praying, forgive, if you have anything against anyone, so that your Father also who is in heaven may forgive you your trespasses" (Mark 11:25, ESV).

~Prayer~

Father, I thank You for everything that You have allowed me to go through. Thank You for every trial and tribulation that helped me be the person You called me to be. I am grateful for Your faithfulness to me as a Father.

Chapter 8

For My Good

Life can present experiences that will be the most significant tests and lessons we will face. Many will challenge our ability to see anything positive in them. However, God has a divine way of transforming traumatizing encounters into a beneficial ending. The price of crucifixion for our salvation, for example, was by all counts traumatizing for Jesus. While Jesus prayed in the Garden of Gethsemane for this experience to pass him by, he nonetheless submitted himself to his Father's will for our benefit (Matthew 26:39, KJV).

A few years ago, God whispered a message to me that I preached, "It Will All Add Up." Through this message, He let me know that I was going through something for a greater purpose. The Apostle James declared in James 1:2-4 (ESV), we should count it all joy when we go through trials. This will build character, steadfastness, and increase your faith. You will be ready for God's greater purpose in your life. Therefore, you should seek to find the purpose of the trials that you have or will face.

I once was in a relationship that caused me to have a nervous breakdown. After losing my mind, I was confused and in a very dark place of despair. I was entangled with someone that messed with my mental stability. At first, I thought I had found true love. His charm and deeds were luring yet deceitful, and before I knew it, I was in love with the wrong man. My self-esteem was so low that I allowed myself to stay in a relationship that was a secret. What I thought was the best thing that had ever happened to me was the worst thing for me. Ladies be careful of who you allow in your life when you try to substitute for who is not there. Being in a relationship with someone that was not for me almost cost me my sanity. Thank God for his keeping power; because of it, I overcame.

One day, I went with the congregation to another church to sing in the choir. I remember it just like it was yesterday, although it was over twenty years ago. The minister of music from that church began to play the organ and sing, "No weapon formed against me shall prosper." The melody and the anointing that was on his voice began to minister to me. I received deliverance on that day. I thank God for the anointing in other people's lives that can set others free. After I left the service, I felt so much different than when I arrived. God used that man to destroy yokes in my life. I later requested for him to come to the church that I was attending, but it didn't end up happening.

Many years passed, but I never forgot about my life-changing experience at that church. God is so awesome. That same man married me on August 27, 2016. Yes, look at what God did. He sent me a man who feared God; only He could have made that happen. He sent Bobby Arrington into my life as my soulmate, and I knew it. After dating for seven years, he proposed to me. He married me despite all my flaws, past, and my four children. God knows who we need and what we need in our lives. After being rejected by the men I conceived children with, God sent me the right man to be a father in our household. Bob accepted this great task and faced it head-on.

God makes no mistakes; he knows who we need in our life, and when we need it too. God allowed me to lose my mind to give me the new mind I needed to break free from the enemy and receive a Christ-like mind. It was His perfect will for me to go through the things I went through, including all the broken relationships that I experienced.

When I got married to my husband, it was hard for my daughters to accept. They were not used to a man being in our home. I often feared that he would walk away just like the others because, at one point, things got very rough. My daughters also did not know how to embrace a father figure. It was unfamiliar to them. Thanks be to God that he was a God-fearing man. He honored his commitment to me.

During the difficult times, he would encourage me and constantly remind us all that he would never leave. He showed love in the midst of the bitterness that presented itself. He loved the Lord and fellow worshippers. We could worship God together right in our room. Through our moments of worship, it released the power of God and love in our home.

Love can change things if you let it. Love is so powerful. God is love. "He that loveth not knoweth not God; for God is love." (1 John 4:8, KJV).

Finally, things started looking different in our house. My oldest daughter started to accept him and respected the love he had for me. They built their own relationship, and he often gave her advice. He was so amazing. God also created a special bond between him and my youngest daughter, Serenity.

When we first met, she was two years old. He accepted her and treated her as his own from day one. It was confusing to him how a man could walk away from his own child. He spent so much time with her, supporting her as she grew. Every event she had, he was front and center. He nurtured her and gave her advice as she began to experience growing pains. She knew she could depend on her daddykins.

They would talk about everything. He wanted to know who her friends were and checked on how her daily encounters were. He taught her how to use her singing voice. He coached her on how to play sports and pushed her to do her best academically. He cheered her on and motivated her every time he had a chance to. He treated her like a royal princess and made time to take her to nice restaurants. Bobby showed her a father's love. She was so fortunate to have him in her life, always reminding her that she is an amazing girl.

A few weeks before her twelfth birthday, he took her into the studio to record a song he had written entitled "Amazing Girl." He wanted to get this done so that it could be released on her birthday, which he had promised her. He always did the best he could to keep his word. He wanted to fulfill his promise, and he did. A father will always do what he can for his child no matter what the circumstances are. He didn't let anything stop him from doing what he wanted to do for Serenity.

The recording was a success and was released on her birthday. Who could have known that he would pass away on that very same day! The pain that hit my heart and my mind all at the same time made me feel like I could not go on. I struggle with writing this because it is painful to understand. In life, some things we will not understand. What I do know is that Bob is with the Father. He loved the Lord, and when the Lord came for him, he was ready. This is the comfort that I hold on to knowing that he is resting with the Lord.

~Prayer~

Lord, I am calling on Your name, knowing that You are always there to rescue me. I am grateful that You have been faithful to me. I trust that You were with me every step of the way. It was Your presence that helped me along the way, and I thank You.

Chapter 9

Through It All

When I realized God had set me free, my spirit was grateful. However, before my deliverance, I felt hopeless, walked around with my head down, and took on a woe-is-me mentality. Feeling fatherless, I immersed myself in self-pity. Now it was time for God's glory to be revealed in my life. The truth is my Father was with me all along. I had to realize that I was victorious. I made it through it all. All of the heartache and pain that I endured did not kill me. It made me stronger!

My old mindset was one of defeat. But my renewed mind and spirit thought on the things of God, which "created a new self after the likeness of God in true righteousness and holiness" (Ephesians 4:22-24, ESV). He delivered me from and given me power over the snares of the enemy. I can speak into someone's life to set them free from what once had a hold over me because "we are more than conquerors through him that loved us (Romans 8:37, KJV)." Regardless of what you have gone through, you can overcome grief and live free from the pain caused when whoever walked away from you. Now it is time for you to realize that.

The anointing on my life came through my struggles and triumph. This didn't come easy, but God used it all to empower me. I am grateful for what God our Father did for me – His grace rescued me when I was trapped in bondage. Whatever God allows you to go through, don't resent it or Him. Understand that your suffering is for the will of God that will empower you with an anointing tailor-made to make you effective in your preordained ministry. "But we have this treasure in earthen vessels, that the excellency of the power may be of God, and not of us" (2 Corinthians 4:7, KJV). The tough times you have faced, others have gone through as well. When someone comes across your path, seeking an answer to similar problems, God can use your experiences to help them. This is your opportunity to tell others of God's goodness.

Walking around, feeling sorry for yourself hinders your victory. Yes, it's true, I wanted my father, and I felt rejected, but I survived without my biological father because my spiritual Father was keeping me. If I continued to walk around, being offended by the absence of my father, I would have lost out completely. We cannot stay offended forever by what others have done to us. The Bible tells us a person's wisdom yields patience; "...and it is his glory to pass over a transgression." (Proverbs 19:11, KJV).

Don't stay offended too long by what others have done to cause you pain. If Jesus remained offended, He would not have completed His mission. We can't let what others have done to stop us from being the best person we could be. No one should have the power to strip us of our right to be healthy and whole.

Don't allow yourself to be stuck in the seat of despair. You can live without a father or a mother, but you cannot live without the Father. Our heavenly Father gave us life, and we need Him in order to breathe and live. As you began to accept the Father's will for your life and understand that your life has purpose and destiny determined by God, you release the power of victory over your life. The chains of bondage begin to fall. Shackles are loosed, and you are set free from hurt, pain, disappointment, and despair. You are free to embrace the worry-free life. Once you know that you have God in your life, nothing and no one can defeat you. Regrets and voids are buried with no way of resurrecting.

There was much I went through, but the grace of God, my Father, was with me then and continues to keep me now. As I searched for love and acceptance, God was patient with me. Through it all, God loved me and did not give up on me. As I stated previously, this book, I have a Father, and He was with me all the time, but I knew of Him, but I didn't have a personal relationship with Him. God is calling you unto Himself because He wants to be your Father too.

He wants you to get to know Him to have a better understanding of who you are in Christ and become a better you. The more you spend time with Him, the more you will get to know Him. Read the word of God; it will tell you all about Him. The Holy Bible is a book of guidance and revelation. There is no question unanswered in His word.

As my relationship grew closer to the Lord, I grew stronger as a woman. My life changed for the better.

I began to walk in the direction God chose for me, with His word lighting my feet and my path (Psalm 119:105, KJV). The light of His word brought me into a place of victory over depression regarding my absentee father. It opened the door to a deeper understanding of who I was and what I was called to do. It revealed my purpose and put me among people that helped to nurture the gifts that God had placed in me. The result was my ordination as an Evangelist, whereby I have been spreading the gospel ever since.

When I didn't know my father, I didn't know who I was. I was searching for a man that I thought I needed. While I was searching for him, I was walking away from myself and God. I was distracted from having a relationship with God the Father. Now, I have a new perspective. No longer will I allow pain to trap me and keep me hostage. I no longer have to look for any man for love. The cycle is broken. When I need help, I seek the Father. Isaiah 55:6 (KJV) tells us, "Seek ye the LORD while he may be found, call ye upon him while he is near."

If you feel rejected or abandoned and feel like something is missing in your life, let God take control of your situation. Let God into your heart and heal the brokenness while protecting you from future heartache. If it's broken, He can heal it. "The LORD is nigh unto them that are of a broken heart; and saveth such as be of a contrite spirit" (Psalm 34:18, NIV). Above all else, "keep thy heart with all diligence; for out of it are the issues of life" (Proverbs 4:23, KJV).

The devil wants you to walk around feeling like you are fatherless, but the devil is a liar. The Bible says in Psalm 27:10 (ESV), "For my father and my mother have forsaken me, but the LORD will take me in." God's word is true. I am a living witness. If you are looking for love, search no more. God is love, and He is your Father. And so, we know and rely on the love God has for us. When I realized how much God loved me, I embraced Him and accepted Him and His love in my life.

Only God could cause me to walk victoriously after all I had been through. I hope that you, too, will trust God and receive your healing, walk in victory, and accept our Father into your life.

Chapter 10

Losing A Father

Losing a father can be devastating. It was painful when my stepfather passed away. My family still mourns the loss of a great man. No longer will we have that human being who was a protector, a great advice giver, and a provider. I vividly recall the day he transitioned from this life to his heavenly home. It was warm outside, but chills flowed through our households. When the call came in, I screamed in disbelief instantly, wondering how we could go on without him in our lives. The man that watched over us took care of us, fed, and nurtured us. It was hard to process the fact that he was gone on the morning of July 2, just like that! At the hospital, his lifeless body laid in the hospital room. In the hall outside the room, sounds of cries of pain and despair rang out relentlessly.

Those who had their father in their life may find it challenging to live without the presence of the family hero. It is times like these that we reflect on how important it is to have a father. Drowning your sorrows with alcohol and partaking in chemical substances are not healthy methods of healing. If you are having a hard time coping with the loss of your father, depend on God, the Father. He is willing to help, comfort, and give you sustaining permanent healing. Trusting God when you are burdened with grief is really the only way your broken heart can be properly mended. I have found the following scriptures to begin the healing process: "The LORD is nigh unto them that are of a broken heart; and saveth such as be of a contrite spirit (Psalm 34:18, KJV)". "And I will pray the Father, and he shall give you another Comforter, that he may abide with you forever" (John 14:16, KJV).

Those who cannot relate to having a father may only have feelings of resentment or bitterness with any thoughts about a father figure. It may seem foolish to believe in something or someone if you have a lack of trust. *How can I believe in something that was not available to me?* In this situation, it is understandable how a person would have a hard time connecting with a spiritual father. It may seem easier not to need or want a father. It could feel like having a father is unnecessary. The devil is a liar. It was the Father that gave your life, without which you would not exist.

"And the LORD God formed man of the dust of the ground and breathed into his nostrils the breath of life; and man became a living soul (Genesis 2:7 KJV)."

Circumstances can make us focus on our hurt and pain, blinding us from the truth. For this very reason, many people choose not to believe in God, our Father. But the word of God says in Colossians 1:16 (KJV), "For by him were all things created, that are in heaven, and that are in earth, visible and invisible, whether they be thrones, or dominions, principalities, or powers: all things were created by him, and for him."

We must seek the will of the Lord concerning our lives to be obedient to the Father. *How can you know what is acceptable to Him if you are not aware of His thoughts and plans concerning you?* Jeremiah 29:11 (KJV) says, "For I know the thoughts that I think toward you, saith the LORD, thoughts of peace, and not of evil, to give you an expected end." The word lets us know that God is the author and finisher of our faith. He is our Creator; he is our Father. I hope and trust that you will receive the Father in your life.

Testimony Notes

Testimony _____

_____

_____

_____

_____

_____

_____

_____

_____

_____

_____

_____

_____

_____

Testimony _____

_____

_____

_____

_____

_____

_____

_____

_____

_____

_____

_____

Testimony _____

_____

_____

_____

_____

_____

_____

_____

_____

_____

_____

_____

_____

Testimony _____

_____

_____

_____

_____

_____

_____

_____

_____

_____

_____

_____

_____

Testimony _____

_____

_____

_____

_____

_____

_____

_____

_____

_____

_____

_____

_____

_____

Testimony _____

_____

_____

_____

_____

_____

_____

_____

_____

_____

_____

_____

_____

Testimony _____

_____

_____

_____

_____

_____

_____

_____

_____

_____

_____

_____

Testimony _____

_____

_____

_____

_____

_____

_____

_____

_____

_____

_____

_____

Testimony _____

_____

_____

_____

_____

_____

_____

_____

_____

_____

_____

_____

Testimony _____

_____

_____

_____

_____

_____

_____

_____

_____

_____

_____

_____

_____

Testimony _____

_____

_____

_____

_____

_____

_____

_____

_____

_____

_____

_____

Testimony _____

_____

_____

_____

_____

_____

_____

_____

_____

_____

_____

_____

Testimony _____

_____

_____

_____

_____

_____

_____

_____

_____

_____

_____

_____

_____

Testimony _____

_____

_____

_____

_____

_____

_____

_____

_____

_____

_____

_____

_____

Testimony _____

_____

_____

_____

_____

_____

_____

_____

_____

_____

_____

_____

_____

Testimony _____

_____

_____

_____

_____

_____

_____

_____

_____

_____

_____

_____

Testimony _____

_____

_____

_____

_____

_____

_____

_____

_____

_____

_____

_____

_____

_____

Testimony _____

_____

_____

_____

_____

_____

_____

_____

_____

_____

_____

_____

Testimony _____

_____

_____

_____

_____

_____

_____

_____

_____

_____

_____

_____

Testimony _____

_____

_____

_____

_____

_____

_____

_____

_____

_____

_____

_____

_____

Testimony _____

_____

_____

_____

_____

_____

_____

_____

_____

_____

_____

_____

Testimony _____

_____

_____

_____

_____

_____

_____

_____

_____

_____

_____

_____

Testimony _____

_____

_____

_____

_____

_____

_____

_____

_____

_____

_____

_____

Testimony _____

_____

_____

_____

_____

_____

_____

_____

_____

_____

_____

_____

_____

Testimony _____

_____

_____

_____

_____

_____

_____

_____

_____

_____

_____

_____